Spirits and Oxygen

SPIRITS AND OXYGEN

Yolanda Coulaz

Yolanda Coulaz

PURPLE SAGE PRESS
Deposit, New York

SPIRITS AND OXYGEN

Copyright © 2003
by Yolanda Coulaz

All rights reserved

ISBN 0-9740011-0-4

Except for brief quotes used in articles and reviews, no part of this book may be reproduced by any means without the permission of the publisher.

Cover photograph by Yolanda Coulaz
Cover design by czu design
Author photograph by Roy P. Coulaz

Published by
PURPLE SAGE PRESS
172 Blueberry Drive
Deposit, New York 13754

Printed in the United States of America

Acknowledgments

Grateful acknowledgement is made to the following periodicals and anthologies in which these poems first appeared or are awaiting publication:

Farmingdale Observer: "You"
Long Island Quarterly: "From Brooklyn to Babylon"
The Lyric: "Why?"
North Shore Woman's Newspaper: "Cool, Cotton Comfort"
PKA's Advocate: "I Am"
Partners In Verse: "A Poem for Roy," "After Midnight," "Burned," "I Am," "Journey," "Player," "Sore," "You"
Performance Poets Literary Review Vol. 5: "You"
Performance Poets Literary Review Vol. 6: "Cool, Cotton Comfort"
Performance Poets Literary Review Vol. 7: "Sonnet for a Teacher"
The Poet's Art: "I'll See the Sun Again," "My Mother's Vase," "Real Love," "Resolution," "There Is a Way"

My deepest gratitude to the following writers for their generous responses and encouragement: Susan Astor, Colette Inez, and George Wallace; and for their additional generosity in providing editorial assistance, I would like to especially thank Vince Clemente, Anna DiBella, Norbert Krapf, Patti Tana, and my mentor Maxwell Corydon Wheat, Jr., author of **Following Their Star: Poems of Christmas and Nature**.

Thank you to: Minerva T. Bloom, author of **Passion's Kiss**, for her publishing pointers; and Cliff Bleidner, Performance Poets Association coordinator, for giving me my first of many opportunities to *speak* my poetry.

Many thanks to my family, friends, and fellow poets for their support.

*for my husband, Roy,
my spirits and oxygen*

*...through sunlight
and moonbeams,
laughing at fears,
erasing the tears,
embracing what's left
of our dreams.*

Contents

Foreword by Vince Clemente	15
I Am	19
Inside Out	20
Poet's Migraine	21
Night Schemes	22
A Dream at 4 a.m.	23
Addiction	24
Reflection	25
Insomnia	26
In Shadows	27
Why?	28
As He Slips Away	29
Mercy	30
Numb	31
Lost in Twilight	32
Restless	33
Depression	34
Promises	35
Fat	36
All the Pretty Flowers	37
Breakdown	38
Backslide	39
The Oven Door	40
I'll See the Sun Again	41
Beginnings	42
Resolution	43
Journey	44
In My Car	45
After School Special	46
First Time	48
Time	49
The Girl Next Door	50
Elephant Walk	52
Three Haiku	53
Got Milk?	54
Running with Boys	55

Underground Writer	56
City Girl	57
On Thin Ice	58
Innocent Bystander	59
The Stranger	60
Influenza	62
Latino Legacy	63
Moon Shine	64
Sweet Sixteen	65
Motherless Child	66
Spirits and Oxygen	68
Cool, Cotton Comfort	69
Player	70
Sore	71
'Til Death Do Us Part	72
Eve	73
Empty Smiles	74
Burned	75
From Brooklyn to Babylon	77
Lucky's Tale	78
Sonnet for a Friend	79
Sonnet for a Teacher	80
Season of the Scarecrow	81
Maiden	82
Impatiens in Autumn	83
Daydreaming in March	84
There Is a Way	85
Dandelion	86
Wildflower	87
Absence of Blue	88
Summer Storm	89
Where the Poems Wait	90
Holding On	91
Resurrected	92
Morning of Peace	93
September Sunset	94
Auras of Ontario	95
December Dawn	96
Quarter Moon	97
Winter Sand	98

Mud	99
On the Last Day of the First Month	100
All I Really Want	101
A Different View	102
Leaving Long Island	103
Cleaning Day	104
Hanging Laundry	105
Witness	106
You	107
Hunger	108
Eating the Mango	109
Peanut Butter Dreams	110
Blueberries	111
Fire and Ice	112
Granite	113
In a Dream	114
Mother	115
The Silence of the Flowers	116
Condolence	117
Aftershock	118
Still a Boy at Thirty-Three	119
Tough as Tony	120
Thanksgiving, Route 110 South	122
Pros and Cons of Christmas	123
She Loved Roses	124
Letter to My Father	125
Silk Scarf	126
My Mother's Vase	127
It's Just a Box	128
Lost Rewards	129
After Midnight	130
Real Love	131
A Poem for Roy	132
My Husband	133
These Are the Times	134
This August Night	135
A Weekend without You	136
Afterword by Susan Astor	139
About the Author	141

Foreword

Such a pleasure to encounter such a fine poet, the one who writes, "I cannot turn back, / not now. / I've come this far..." And "far" Yolanda Coulaz has traveled, as along with Theodore Roethke, she insists, "Lord! Hear me and hear me out this day: / From me to Thee's a long and a terrible way." She makes the journey: through city, her descent into place and self, "hanging by a strap," speeding through "tenement aromas," past "character in crucifix and scars / preaching at the rail / peering through the turnstile bars." She has no Virgil to guide her in her descent, her rhumb line, simply compass of her heart, and back from a descent with "No sutures / to close / my wounds. / They will heal / on their own," indeed, the poet as Witness, as Courage-Teacher, one willing to risk everything for song.

She is also poet of suburban America, "Inhaling this sooty school bus breeze," that very place where she found those fruits of the primary glances, those seminal moments, as in the volume's title poem, "Spirits and Oxygen," where a teen-ager, "We'd cut school, hang out and get high / at the handball courts in Peck Park," where these castaways would "...sit for hours, reciting poetry / ...talk about the mystery / of memories we hadn't yet made." In this corner in America, where no one "connects," she found her first songs, the very mystery and evanescence of self.

And she has come far, American city and town, while always porting the lesson found in de Touqueville, that we finally wake to find ourselves locked "within the solitude of our own hearts." And she too has come far in song, indeed poet of the aural imagination: from the romp of sparse, razor-sharp, hammerfall cadences of a poem like "Beginnings," where "I shave layers, / dead skin. / It serves me / no more. / I can't feel!": a poem whose "I can't feel!" rings out across our Republic like Lowell's, "My mind's not right!" Yes, she sings in a range and register that can fine-tune even the demands of a villanelle, in a poem like "Why?,": a poem that moves me to grief's loss and longing as does Elizabeth Bishop's villanelle, "One Art." The poem's refrain, "Why can't I borrow time to give to you?" may serve as the volume's passacaglia, undersong of poignant longing and final victory, the young poet, prayerful before all of creation, that place where "sparrows dare to soar where eagles flew, / And sky can birth a rainbow from the grey." *Reverential* may not be too strong a word to describe such a sense of life's design, the God-head's handiwork.

I'm pleased to report, Yolanda Coulaz is a poet who must be read again and again, one whose range and vision, whose hard-won wisdom remind us of just what it is to be human, whose poems locate the prayer behind the prayer, make us whole again.

–Vince Clemente
Sag Harbor, New York
May 2003

Vince Clemente, a SUNY English Professor Emeritus, is a poet-biographer, whose books include **John Ciardi: Measure of the Man, Paumanok Rising**, and eight volumes of verse, one of which, **A Place for Lost Children**, is a text used at the University of Wales at Swansea. He lives in Sag Harbor with his wife, Ann, and serves as a columnist for *The Sag Harbor Express*. **The Vince Clemente Papers** are now part of the Rush Rhees Library, Department of Rare Books & Collections of Rochester University. His most recent book of poetry is **Sweeter Than Vivaldi**.

"The poet's country is words and his dominions blank pages"

— Alberto Blanco

I AM

In a wood and wicker rocking chair
in the corner of my garden room
where all the leaves are green,
and I am blue.

I come here when I hurt,
when the pain becomes the dirt
that won't wash off with hope and water.

I am the distant, detached daughter
floating on the outskirts of a family.
No room for this bad apple on the tree.

I am a seed so hastily hurled,
hovering on the outskirts of a world
where no one cares,
where someone stares
and waits for something great
to come from me.

I am a tiny, shining star.
No place for this small speck
on such a spacious planet.
Just a flaming ball of dust,
incarnate dreams and lust
glowing in the air above the granite,
grey and cold.

Where white winds blow
no open arms await below.
Here I sit and think
and never know
who I am.

INSIDE OUT

Always on the outside,
looking in.
My vision fogged
by mists of
disillusionment.
My face pressed
up against the pane
of shattered schemes.

Always on the inside,
looking out.
My fingers cling
to sills with
chipped lead paint
and rotted wood
of broken dreams.

Always on the flip-side,
falling short,
playing to the deaf
and dancing for the blind,
singing to the music
that plays only in my mind.

Always on the downside,
looking up,
grabbing at the ladder
of my fate,
reaching for the rungs
too weak to bear my weight.

POET'S MIGRAINE

Pieces of poetry,
Tattered and torn,
Whispers of words
All withered and worn,
Throbbing within the walls
Of my head.
I can't stop this pain
Until they are said,
Until they're all dead.

These are the thoughts
That howl through my head,
That bother my brain,
Until they are dead,
Until they're all said.

NIGHT SCHEMES

in dreaming
I am I
and I am he
I am myself
and I am you
and I am she

I am what I fear
what I hate
I am the demons
of my past
I am my fate

I am the cats
I am the dogs
I am the angels
and the gods

in dreams
I am the meek
I am the mild
I am my loves
and I am wild

A DREAM AT 4 A.M.

it's 4 a.m.
4 a.m. and all i can do is dream
dream of men
men in uniform and me
me in uniform and an old woman
an old woman, german
german and inexperienced
inexperienced and afraid
afraid and with me
me? i'm not afraid. well
well, i wasn't
i wasn't until
until i met the old woman
the old woman and the men
men in uniform
in a dream
at 4 a.m.

ADDICTION

She lies in wait
within,
hibernates
beneath the skin.

Patiently poised,
she wages war.
This saboteur
strikes fierce.

Her arrows pierce
the hungry heart.

REFLECTION

Tanned Italian olive skin.
Flowing hair of cinnamon.

Marble eyes of chestnut-brown.
Full lips bent into a frown.

INSOMNIA

Face to face
with the mechanical beast
that lives on my wall.

Awaiting the fall of day
and the rise of night,
like hunter and prey,
we engage in the game.
The outcome is always the same.

The hands of this demon
work their way into my weakness,
enter the tunnel of sound
and pound
the sensitive skin
of this organ,
drumming their fingers,
humming the dirge of darkness.

Exhaustion incites a retreat.
Aprons of skin
drape heavily over my eyes.
I remain under cover,
fear I'll not reap
the sweet spoils of sleep.

The wake of dawn brings a truce.
Light from the east salutes
the enemy face, and he smiles.

IN SHADOWS

I photograph you
while you sleep,
when all we share
is ozone and oxygen,
and breath and pulse become one
in an otherwise empty bed,
where aspirations are conceived
and moonbeams frame your face.
I linger in this place,
await the dawn
when sunlight
breaks the dream.

WHY?

If black of night can turn to morning blue,
And sunlight can create another day,
Why can't I borrow time to give to you?

Why can't I find a way to make things new,
Erase the tears and take your pain away,
If black of night can turn to morning blue?

If dust of day gives way to evening dew,
And God hears every word that people say,
Why can't I borrow time to give to you?

Why is there nothing more that they can do
And nothing left for us except to pray,
If black of night can turn to morning blue?

If sparrows dare to soar where eagles flew,
And sky can birth a rainbow from the grey,
Why can't I borrow time to give to you?

If seedlings can survive where wild winds blew,
And grass grows green where children often play,
If black of night can turn to morning blue,
Why can't I borrow time to give to you?

AS HE SLIPS AWAY

It's early February,
just shy of midnight,
and the air reminds my flesh
that winter is still with us.

The world is red
with roses and love poems,
and I am grey as a whisper,
soft as dust.

Shameless in my lack of strength,
I do not harden
for fear that I may shatter
as he slips away.

MERCY

Rhythmic blips,
persistent, insistent.
Loudspeaker words,
muffled and distant.

On borrowed breath,
her chest rises and wanes.
Exhausted blood crawls
through her veins.

With a voice as loud
as my willingness to hear,
she begs for release,
for surrender, for peace.

Her sandpaper skin
absorbs the last tear
from my face.

A trace of my fear remains.
The moment draws near.

A flip of a switch,
a yank of the cord
rend a slow,
steady stream
of sound waves
through the ward.

NUMB

His heart is on hold,
this hollow man.
He remains numb
as he bears
the weight of her hand.

Numb,
he
remains,
as
the
IV
drips
poison
promises
into
her
veins.

Empty inside, he is tin.
He wonders what sin
could have brought
her to this.

LOST IN TWILIGHT

Insulated by the warmth
of freshly fallen snow,
I daydream into dusk.

Sun betrays me to the stars.
My only light, reflections
of the budding moon
off fields of white.

Like the black-tipped underwing
of day's last sleepy seagull,
I fade. I fade into night.

RESTLESS

I sleep within the cold
plaster and paint
of these hollow walls,
where determined winds wail
and rattle the metal and glass
of storm windows.

I place hothouse tulips
and daffodils in dark corners
to chase winter out of this room,
burn incense and candles
and kerosene lamps to remind myself
that this season will, one day,
surrender to spring.

DEPRESSION

It waits
for that one weak moment,
that wisp of a second
when a smile turns to doubt.
It sneaks up from behind.
The target, my mind.

With a gust so abrupt,
it leaps out from the box
with the lock and the key,
that I thought so secure,
buried well within me.

I was sure. I was sure
this monster was dead,
that my being could hold it
and keep it from charging
back into my head.

I was wrong. I was wrong.
There's a war going on.
Each battle, I fight to the death
and with every last breath
of what's left of my reason.

PROMISES

Somebody told me if I behaved
And lived my life doing as I was told
I'd never go hungry, never be cold.
Salvation was there for me to behold.

Somebody told me this road was paved.
I didn't know I'd have to muddy my pride,
Or that, only to me, the rules applied.
I didn't know that Somebody lied.

Somebody told me that I'd be saved.
I didn't know I'd have to sell my soul
To the living in lieu of the man in the hole.
Somebody's words have taken their toll.

FAT

No man will ever love you if you're that.
She knows it's true 'cause mama never lies.
She prays her flesh will never turn to fat.
The scale reveals the truth, and mama cries.

She knows it's true 'cause mama never lies.
She starves herself for days, and then she cheats.
The scale reveals the truth, and mama cries.
Intention cast aside, she eats and eats.

She starves herself for days, and then she cheats.
She sinfully succumbs to every urge.
Intention cast aside, she eats and eats.
Mindlessly, she gorges then the purge.

She sinfully succumbs to every urge.
She prays her flesh will never turn to fat.
Mindlessly, she gorges then the purge.
No man will ever love you if you're that.

ALL THE PRETTY FLOWERS

Mother peels leaves
of Shasta daisies,
black-eyed Susans,
purple coneflower.

She trims these blooms
to fit her Aztec vase,

slims stems to fit
societal displays,

makes them perky and petite
to please the eyes of men.

BREAKDOWN

Ominous and opaque,
the obstacles appear,
speedbumps
of blacktop and tar.
I blink. I freeze
with accelerated fear.

The malignancy grows.
Now it shows.
There's a scar.

Where it bled,
it comes to a head.
There's no turning back.
I am under attack.
I crash, and I crack.

Stalled, I remain
in the comfort of black.
No joy, no pain,
just the numb
of emotional lack.

BACKSLIDE

I slip and fall,
backslide again,
into the arms
of my old friend.

This pain goes deep,
cuts to the bone.
I can't escape
my comfort zone.

THE OVEN DOOR

I sit on the floor,
look at myself
as I'd never before.

I'd been on the shelf
for so long.
The vinyl is soft to the touch.
It feels warm.

This looking glass,
spotted, foggy, and grey.
I see only shadows of me.
They portray
no details, no color, no form.

Like un-caressed clay,
it all looks the same,
a murky matte finish.
No gloss, no glow, no name.
No one to blame.

There's nothing to show,
nothing to know.
No ideas, just tears
slapping, tapping kitchen tile.

Exhausted fans drown
the sound
in this antiseptic exile.

I'LL SEE THE SUN AGAIN

I lift the blinds,
draw them again.

A minute or two has passed,
and I think it's the last
I will see of the sun.

I crack open a slat, just one,
enough to see
teardrops and sleet slapping pavement,
sidewalks of stone and slate and cement.

The mighty trees lament.
They all but cave
under the onslaught of water.

They cry
in empathy for me.

I heave a sigh,
knowing
I will see the sun again.

BEGINNINGS

I cut myself
craving.
The razor
too sharp,
I jump off
the edge
and dive in.

I shave layers,
dead skin.
It serves me
no more.
I can't feel!

I cut loose,
and it falls
to the floor
at my heel,
and I bleed.

The pain of
skin thinning,
raw flesh,
I reveal
to mesh
with my future.

No sutures
to close
my wounds.
They will heal
on their own.

RESOLUTION

I cannot turn back,
not now.
I've come this far,
don't know how.

I've gazed into
amusement park mirrors,
cut through
the binders and fillers,
fallen before,
through the hole in the floor
that I've paced
with a bloody, bare foot.

I've polished away
at this dirty ashtray,
through the tarnish,
the grime, and the soot.

I cannot turn back.

JOURNEY

I cannot realize
my dreams and fears,
cannot recognize
what causes tears.

I cannot reason life.
There is no sense.
There are so many stones.
Grabbing at what's left
of innocence,
I take this jagged path
to walk alone.

If you come along
I'll understand.
I'll find my way.
I'll take your hand
through sunlight
and moonbeams,
laughing at fears,
erasing the tears,
embracing what's left
of our dreams.

IN MY CAR

Yesterday I drove somewhere,
hoping I might find you there.
Today I am nowhere
without you.

Tomorrow I'll go wandering,
driving everywhere,
knowing I'll be wondering
about you.

AFTER SCHOOL SPECIAL

Maybe it was more than spare change
or college money that I was after
in my part-time supermarket checkout days.

Those boys didn't go to my school.
They were locked away, sheltered
behind stained-glass windows
and dark oak doors,
hidden within the walls
of single-gender,
parochial academies,
those ripe young men
with their seductively innocent
stock-boy smiles.

Ray was my buddy
until he tried to kiss me.
Eddie was quite a bit older,
and you could never be sure
whose side he was on.

Jimmy played bartender
at the makeshift tavern,
back behind the produce aisle,
camouflaged by crates
of cantaloupe, corn, and cabbage.

Sipping a sloe gin fizz
and scents of strip steaks searing
on the shrink-wrap machine
tempted my taste buds.

Maybe it was more
than a bite of beef that I wanted.

John was the one
with those chestnut-brown,
Labrador eyes.
He was the one in my dreams,
the one who locked my coat
in his locker *purely by accident*
on that cold winter night.

Maybe it was more
than my coat that he wanted.

Too young and naïve
to imagine anything more,
I wondered how his lips
would taste, shaken not stirred.

Maybe it was more
than his lips that I wanted.

FIRST TIME

It was supposed to be the puppy kind,
the hand-holding, heavy-petting,
weak-in-the-knees kind,
the clumsy, stumbling, bumbling,
groping-hands-of-adolescent-innocence kind,
the pimple-faced, missed-the-mouth,
caught-the-chin kind,
the wide-eyed, tongue-tied,
mumbling-all-the-wrong-words kind,
the giggles and wiggles of peach-fuzz,
baby-fat, flesh-upon-flesh kind.
It was supposed to be that.

It was the hand-over-mouth,
sickening-stench-of-Sweet-Honesty-
sweat-and-stale-smoke-saliva kind,
the two-hundred-pounds-of-beer-bellied,
rib-cage-crushing-the-lungs,
can't-catch-a-breath kind,
should've-listened-to-what-mama-said kind,
wish-I-was-dead kind,
the stubble-scraped-skin-of-a-cheek kind,
pain-in-the-bones, ripped-shirt-reminder kind.
It was that kind.

TIME

I
took
it
by
the
hand
today
caressed
it
cajoled
it
held
it
as
it
slipped
away

THE GIRL NEXT DOOR

When we first met, her eyes
held apprehension and distrust.
Easily mistaken for a bitch, she was,
with her white-boot strut.
Just looking for attention, a little love
less the customary conditions.

Once she let me inside
I knew I'd fallen hard.
I do not know her name,
and so I call her Angel.
This is a first for me. I usually
keep company with the boys.

I despise the man she's with.
He never touches her,
never gives her what she needs.
She comes to me when he is gone
but never stays more than moments.
I want so much to take her away.

Although her life is not good,
it is her sameness, her stasis.
How can I make her see
that life would be better with me,
unless she takes the chance, the leap
from comfort to the cold of new waters?

I long to caress her russet-red hair,
to feel her head, once again, on my thigh.
I want nothing more than the warmth of
her touch on a cold winter night.

One day I will move away,
to another town, another time.
I will take her with me,
and no one will be the wiser
when they see me walking
in the cool evening breeze
with three dogs instead of two.

ELEPHANT WALK

Neck to collar, collar
to lead, lead to palm.
Palm to lead, lead
to collar, collar to neck.

We follow this trail,
my dogs and I.
The oldest first,
my Akita-golden-
Great Dane mix,
my Bear.

I in the middle,
my arms outstretched
like trunk and tail.
My arms stretched out
like some archaic,
medieval torture.

The youngest last,
the baby of the herd,
my little pitbull, Petie.

Like a proper pack
of pachyderms
we walk this walk.

THREE HAIKU

Frisbees cut through clouds
Dogs rebound off amber sand
Vision gently soars

***

Lightning ignites sky
Thunder roars in the distance
My spine slightly stirs

***

I see the Monarch
It mambos with milkweeds
Memory flutters

GOT MILK?

Leading authorities
might attribute
my strong skeletal system
to my teenage years,
those years I spent hung over,
guzzling gallons of milk
at the refrigerator door.
I read somewhere that it has
just the right combination
of electrolytes.
Perhaps that's why I craved it,
couldn't get enough of it,
after a night out
or a day of mowing the lawn.

I never broke one of these 206 bones.
Not when I was hit from behind
by that nearsighted doctor
who didn't even pay
to repair my bent bicycle frame.
Not on Easter Sunday
when I fell down
my parents' cellar stairs
with a bucket of brown, soapy water
and two wood folding chairs.
Not even when my friend Cheryl
sideswiped a tree,
with my arm hanging out
the passenger side window,
on a warm Woodstock night.

RUNNING WITH BOYS

My hands were small,
but I beat them all
with my tomboy ways.

I beat them both,
those tough Slavic twins,
in our pre-teen days;
zero losses, all wins.

Then hormones
kicked in;
I grew breasts,
they grew biceps,
and both stood in the way
of my winning
that Indian game.

UNDERGROUND WRITER

Hanging by a strap,
cradled in aluminum enclosure,
absorbing all the crap
that flashes by.

Auras of ecliptic exposure,
posted papers, numbered maps.
A pregnant woman's twins
begin to cry.

Queer character in crucifix and scars,
preaching at the rail,
peering through the turnstile bars.

Tenement aromas,
commuters in their comas.

Reverberating rapping
echoes on the tracks.
Truant teens wear egos
on their backs.
Silently I slip between
the crevices and cracks.

CITY GIRL

She reads cheap paperbacks
and bibles and takes them
at their word, wears black
and lives on caffeine,
cigarettes and stress.

Her nails are nubs;
cuticles, ragged and raw;
hair, Midnight #36.

Her skin is pale
in sky scraper shadows,
and she is lean
for lack of transportation.

She eats soft pretzels
soaked in humidity,
seasoned with salt
and carbon monoxide,
searches for something
in subways and taverns,
and she doesn't read
the funnies anymore.

ON THIN ICE
(After an article by Tom Walker)

Ursus maritimus: Bear of the Sea.

He stands
on a long spit of land
at Cape Churchill.
Sagging skin,
ecru and ivory fur
drape over bony frame.
Global warming
has left him lacking blubber.

Hunger propels him north.
He jumps floe to floe;
his footing fails, and he plunges
into churning, choppy seas.
Amid rolling pressure ridges
and slamming ice,
the currents hurl him
against glassy blue-green boulders.

On the hunt for ring seal,
walrus, and narwhal,
he fades into misty grey fog
at the Arctic river's mouth
in Hudson Bay.

INNOCENT BYSTANDER

Weighted down by burdens
of some corporate clay
that I have yet to meet.

I am not composed
of hardened carbon steel
with coats of chrome
or cold concrete.

I am not immune to rust.
I will, one day, crack
and turn to dust,

be washed away
with tears of children
not yet born.

And they will mourn,
as I have mourned,
for those who came before
and cared as much as I.

THE STRANGER

He lets me go ahead of him
in housewares.
I hurry past,
but cannot look away.

Wrinkled and unshaven,
he slouches,
crouches at the cutlery,
clutches two knives,
blades still sheathed, sheltered
in their blister-pack plastic
and cardboard cocoons.

He fidgets, fingers the handles
with grainy hands
and dirt-encrusted fingernails.

A blank stare emerges
from beneath his darkened brow,
surrounds me with frigid emptiness.
Blood escapes my hands,
soars to my throat,
leaves my fingers shaken and blue.

I tunnel my way to the counter,
cutting through the thickness
of my thoughts,
finish my business,
rush to the parking lot,
stunned by the blaze
of the two o'clock sun.

I fire up my engine
and drive away,
wonder where and when
I will see him again.
The New York Times,
a post office wall,
the news at ten?

INFLUENZA

With a name like that
you would expect
an Italian opera singer
or some leggy Spanish dancer.

But no.
She is the witch who waits
in the shadows of summer.
She hides in membranes
of the darkness and the dust.

Awakens,
enters with a whisper,
in a breath,
on wings of winter winds.

Her catalyst,
the stale, dry air.
She strikes in my sleep
when I am least aware.

I am her host,
begrudgingly.
We do not dance.
She does not sing to me.

LATINO LEGACY

She came, with her husband,
from Poland with hopes
of a better life
and dreams of a family.

They lived on the corner
of Columbus and Rome,
within the warehouse walls
of cement, cinder block, and brick,
across from the machine shop
where all of the workers
were young and dark.

Her first-born,
fair of hair with milky skin
and sulking eyes of Topaz-blue,
a reflection of his father.

Her second son,
cappuccino complected
with sparkling sable eyes
and silken hair
the color of Colombian coffee
black with a hint of sugar.

MOON SHINE

I see, from behind, the slight bow
of his bony legs outlined
in the rugged denim of his jeans.

I wonder how those stilts
support the rest of him.

Wonder how those gangling,
flanneled limbs find strength
to push a baby carriage.

I wonder who this stranger is
and how he lives his life.

He could be a carbon copy
clone of my old friend.

Could be the original,
had he not drunk himself to death.

SWEET SIXTEEN

Learning of love
on a bench in the park
and the back of a '69
Buick Skylark.

Molested by quaaludes
and alcohol
on an afternoon trip
to the local strip mall.

Checking out goods
at the corner store,
daydreaming, wishing,
wanting for more.

MOTHERLESS CHILD

It's that special cigarette case
with its cherry-smoke
burgundy leather
weathered and worn
in all the right places,
your gift to me
some twenty years ago,
that makes me think of you.

It's that embossed,
pink-painted rose
on the front
and the rivets
along the sides,
all tarnished and oxidized
green at the marriage
of leather and brass,
that make me think of you.

It's that song,
"Green Grass and High Tides"
by The Outlaws
that you dedicated to me
on WLIR on my birthday
some twenty years ago,
that makes me think of you.

It's the smell of mayonnaise,
the way you used it
in the meals you prepared
for your father and brother
when you came home from school,
that makes me think of you,
and the way you'd sneak a spoonful
when the egg salad wasn't looking.

SPIRITS AND OXYGEN

We'd cut school, hang out and get high
at the handball courts in Peck Park,
yards and years away
from the sandbox and swings.

We'd sit for hours, reciting poetry
about condoms and quaaludes,
in a corner booth at the local Bagel Nosh.

I'd smuggle in whiskey
down the front of my jeans,
and we'd slurp seven and sevens
through thick milkshake straws
because alcohol and oxygen
gets you drunker faster
than alcohol alone.
We'd make sure to double
those wax paper cups
so the Seagrams wouldn't seep through.

We'd talk about the mystery
of memories we hadn't yet made,
sing duets out of tune,
memorize every line
from *The Rocky Horror Picture Show*,
and we promised we'd always be friends.

I heard from the sister of a friend of a friend
you're still living somewhere in Queens.

COOL, COTTON COMFORT

I wore him like a tight pair of jeans,
and he looked damn good on me.
It was almost obscene,
that tight pair of jeans.

He didn't fit,
and I was proud of it
and the way they'd stare
at that man I'd wear.
It was almost obscene,
that pair of jeans.

Well, I'm older today,
and I've got a man that fits
like a pair of sweats, heather grey,
and he looks damn good on me.
And that tight pair of jeans?
Well, I threw him away.

PLAYER

I've been dealing double,
causing trouble.

Stealing hearts
is a dangerous part to play.
I portray the queen quite well.

The price of hell
to pay, I walk away.
I drew this fate,
can't play my hand anymore.

I can't see straight,
stumble out the door.
The Jacks and Diamond Jims
don't follow.

Empty and hollow,
I've had enough,
played too rough.
I climb up to street level.
I'm cashed in, stripped, disheveled.

The game is done;
the players have disbanded.
Again, I've come up empty-handed.
I've lost, and no one else has won.

SORE

An ulcer has grown
in the garden where our love once flourished.
There's a hole filled with only the dust
of some seedlings, malnourished.

When she whispers your name
there's a hunger
once satisfied
when we were younger.

When she calls your name there is pain
where a rose should have bloomed.
Where secrets are exhumed,
our sins are all that remain.

'TIL DEATH DO US PART

Days grow tense.
Hours cut layers from the fuse.
He paces, mumbles,
snaps at every word.
She knows there's no turning back.

Eyes sharp, icy hot,
stare burning, blaming.
A sneeze, a twitch,
a breath too deep ignite his rage.
She knows there's no turning back.

His face, once soft as skin,
has turned to steel. He cannot feel a thing.
She wishes to be stone, as hard as he.
She wishes to be free.
And she knows there's no turning back.

Enclosed in the cocoon of a hospital room,
on a dopamine drip, she cannot feel a thing.
Time manipulates her wounds from red
to blue to pale yellow, soft and forgotten.
She knows there's no turning back.

The kitchen floor wears shreds of her clothing
and crusty, black-burgundy scabs.
She buries the clothes in a hole in the yard
and envies the comfort of soil,
scrubs the tile with brush and bleach
and wishes to be clean of him.
And she knows there's no turning back.

She paces, mumbles, waits for his return.
She knows there's no turning back.

EVE

Hardcore
whore,
nucleus
of some
atomic apple
of destruction.
Deployed,
employed
to infiltrate
inflated molecules
of male machines.

EMPTY SMILES

I meet you in a bar,
by chance.
You are with her,
but this is not the woman
you left with long ago.
Her hair, height, features
all changed.

You sit at my booth
uninvited.
I smile at your lady.
Her lips curve upward
at the corners,
but her eyes do not lie.

She is with children,
your children.
A boy with a gremlin grin
removes the contents of my bag,
tears at pages of poetry.
Kewpie doll daughter
discovers my make-up,
masks her face with lipstick,
powder, and blush,
fills in the blanks.
A paint-by-numbers smile.

Morning comes.
I wake in the comfort of a bed
a thousand miles away from you.

BURNED

Awakened by the spectrum of your stare,
Seduced from slumber's safe, secluded dreams,
Bedazzled by your enigmatic glare,
Enticed by bursts of brilliant, blazing beams,
I was burned.

In biting, bitter mists of our dawn,
Tempted by impassioned embrace,
Ecstatically enraptured, I was drawn
To the radiance that was your face.
And I was burned.

With promises of sultry, summer days,
Stripped naked, spirit bare,
Exposed to flaming, fiery, fervent rays,
Lured into your energetic air,
I was burned.

MY BEAR

Starved
by sleet and snow
of the only mother you had known.

Hunted
by late winter winds of lions.

Nurtured
by the warmth of urine and feces.

Plucked
from a womb of blacktop and tar.

Delivered
at my feet, oh un-requested gift.

Metamorphosed
from fur and skin-soaked skeleton
into golden-shepherd-Dane, my guardian.

FROM BROOKLYN TO BABYLON

Mid-August morning,
a time when cicadas die
and sea scallops dance.

There's a scent
of coffee and Clorox
in the air.

Veiled sun
and foggy alabaster moon
share this mourning sky.

On graveled blacktop
caterpillar crawls
like thirsty Bedouin
across Saharan sands.

Once again,
I play God for a friend.

LUCKY'S TALE

There he was, one summer day,
Abandoned in the street.
Each morning I would go outside
To find him at my feet.

He spent some time without a home,
Afraid and on the loose,
Imprisoned by his memories
Of puppyhood abuse.

He took both food and drink from me,
But wouldn't come inside
Until a car sped down the road
And took a turn too wide.

After major surgery
His bones began to mend.
Then I took him home with me,
My little faithful friend.

One day my Lucky dog fell ill,
And there was not a cure.
We tried to do our best for him,
But he could bear no more.

I had just five short years with him.
Our time passed like a breeze.
I knew I had to let my friend
Succumb to this disease.

I could have held him here with me.
That would have been much worse
Than setting Lucky's spirit free
To roam the universe.

SONNET FOR A FRIEND

What is this thing that causes me such pain
That burrows into breast and blood and bone
Where shell of skin and flesh and tear remain?
If not for these I would be air alone.

What is this thing that strikes, that tears apart
Each fiber, every thread of every vein?
These vessels that pump life throughout my heart
Collapse, succumb, surrender to this bane.

This germ has now infected every cell.
For loving precious beast, this price I pay.
I recognize this face; I know it well.
It shows itself each time friends fade away.

Again it plants a seed within my core.
I bid farewell to my best friend once more.

SONNET FOR A TEACHER
(For Maxwell Corydon Wheat, Jr.)

When first our eyes met, into prose I fell,
Transcended to another place and time.
He wears his wisdom and his wit quite well,
Inspires me with reason and with rhyme.

With Spencer Tracy flair and argyle style,
His words seduced me into poetry.
I feel, sometimes, as if I am a child
Cajoled by metaphor and simile.

A bard of modern times, he pens his song.
Parchment bears witness to his serenade.
Into his gentle aura, I am drawn,
And well deserved is this, my accolade.

I pray our fond affair will never end.
He is my muse, my mentor, and my friend.

SEASON OF THE SCARECROW

It is the season of the scarecrow,
Protector of my garden, keeper of the corn,
Guardian of all that dwell below.
His uniform of denim, tattered; flannel, torn.

He towers over stretching, silky stalks,
Alert to uninvited black-winged guests.
Prepared to frighten anything that walks,
He watches over every craggy crest.

It is the season of the scarecrow,
Brave as any sentry to the Queen,
Strong as any bastion I have known,
Keeping safe my fields of gold and green.

MAIDEN

She blooms in hyacinth and marigold,
And when she speaks the wind plays with her hair.
With every breath her beauty they behold.

They follow her, these men both young and old.
They follow her to fields and meadows where
She blooms in hyacinth and marigold.

When maiden smiles her mysteries unfold,
And all the men can do is stop and stare.
With every breath her beauty they behold.

They brave the sun, the wind, the rain, the cold.
Their only gift, to see her standing there.
She blooms in hyacinth and marigold.

They offer her their silver and their gold
And all the silk and satin she can wear.
With every breath her beauty they behold.

She is immortalized in stories told
Of violet eyes and porcelain skin so fair.
She blooms in hyacinth and marigold.
With every breath her beauty they behold.

IMPATIENS IN AUTUMN

Early one October morn,
While walking through a leaf-strewn lawn,
While sparrows sing a mourning song
For all but barren trees,

I come upon a flower fair
Perched amid the maidenhair,
Waving in the autumn air,
Peeking through the leaves.

I gaze upon her rosy blush
Whispering through the dewy hush
Awaiting sharp and bitter rush
Of winter's coming freeze.

She had her time to flourish there.
Once lavish stems, now nearly spare;
Once florid blossoms, almost bare.
So many she had pleased.

DAYDREAMING IN MARCH

Playing past my kitchen picture window
Upon a silken, satin stage of snow,
Cracked and broken pods of seeds
Dance among last season's reeds.

Mustard yellow, marbled mud
And brick red, terra cotta streams
Meld with remains of yesterday,
Swimming with the sun's noon-beams.

Like some potter's clay it lies in wait
While earth and air of coming spring create.
Nurtured by the nature of their winter
April seedlings soon will splinter

Through the cracks of pure white focus.
Lavender, yellow, and creamy crocus,
Pastel pink tulips, and daffodils
Soon will mottle mountainside and hills.

THERE IS A WAY

There is a way the sun bleeds through
The boughs of birch and pine.
She lights the way for all who walk
The path of the divine.

There is a way the sun reflects
Off fur of squirrel and possum.
She warms the earth to spur the growth
Of early springtime blossoms.

There is a way the sun beats down
Upon the crystal lake.
She sneaks in through an open blind
And nudges me to wake.

DANDELION
(For Christine)

Cutting through the concrete cracks
of city streets,
season after season, she endures.

Her rugged roots secure,
anchored in the hidden, fertile soil
that dwells beneath skyscraper feet.

She blooms
amid industrial debris,
despite landscaper surgeries,
unscented, unrelenting,
past plastic potted sceneries
where meticulous gardeners groom.

WILDFLOWER

In a world of blossoms and buds
I am a weed.

A wildflower growing,
sowing seed.

Not in rows, in scattered patterns
marking verdant fields.
No boundaries, no shields.

No shelter from the wind and rain.
They serve to feed.
There is no need to hide.
There is no pain.
Just sun and rain.

ABSENCE OF BLUE

It's 6:00 a.m.
on a Saturday,
and already
I've invested hours
in this misty spring day.

Newscasters and neighbors
complain about clouds
and the coming of rain
and the grey.

Sparrows and squirrels,
begonia and blacktop
are content
in this absence of blue.

The cool in the air
that beachcombers fear
keeps me in my comfort.

Others are sweatered
and chilled,
and I am sleeveless.
I bask in the subnormal
temperatures of this season.

No burn,
no sweat,
no complaints.

SUMMER STORM

moths
click – click
flicking fixtures
beat their brains
lightning ignites
a sun-shy sky
thunder
shatters
my eye

WHERE THE POEMS WAIT

They are in subways
riding the trains,
bundled in backpacks
and briefcases.

They hide
behind the eyes
in planetary whispers.

They are in plain sight
beneath the glass,
just a walk on the wall
in a dream about elbows,
the suede-patched,
comfortable, corduroy kind.

In and out of sleep,
beyond blue,
they swing on stars.

They are under the pillow
with baby teeth and fairy dust.

They are under the bed,
breathing in the world.

HOLDING ON

Just south of Staples
on Secatogue,
gangly wisteria strangles
a small stockade fence,
weeps in shadows
of lavender and leaf.

This wood bag of bones,
worn and washed pale
by a decade of winters,
splinters, broken by time,
sustained by the talons
of its attacker.

Like flesh to its virus,
surrendered, silent, still,
these pickets play host
to their pastel predator.

RESURRECTED

Granite clouds struggle,
cling to canvas
bathed in cerulean blue.

Cobalt waves wield
their foamy white spit of the sea,
invade the unsuspecting calm.

Virgin sky cradles womb
of coral, pink, and violet.

Seagulls hover, as do angels,
witness, as do wise men.

Azure blue gives birth
to infant alabaster sun.

MORNING OF PEACE

It's a strange sky,
slate grey,
ocher at the horizon.

Charcoal chases,
clings to hungry clouds
enormous in their appetite.

Sky sleeps in solace
like a cancer-host
surrendered before capture.

Sun screams–
rays cut through cumulus.

SEPTEMBER SUNSET

I've gazed upon
this perfect
orange orb
for so long now;
I'm almost blind
to shape and form.

Her skin glows
with the color
of my morning
mango's flesh
and begs me
to indulge
in the succulence
that hangs
in the afternoon sky.

She moves
in silence,
descending
to a place
I do not know.

AURAS OF ONTARIO

A lone canoe lingers
amid bulbous boulders,
patiently at rest, an extension
of these ancient, knobby hills.

Earth conducts her symphony.
A paint brush, her baton.

She gasps in the cold October air.
Night transforms its black into dawn.

Maroon mountains fiddle
with soft, supple flesh
of coral, peach, and lavender.

Azure waves awaken,
thrust their baritones;
autumn's chill
returns their song.

And sky strikes up soprano tones
of apricot, amber, and dew.

DECEMBER DAWN

I rush to dress,
to primp, to groom,
bounce from wall
to wall of my room,
glance out my window
and nod to the day.

I'm stopped in my steps
by a vast array –
fuschias, magentas,
most glorious hues.

The lid of my eye
barely scrapes the sky,
reveals the cerulean blue.

QUARTER MOON

A powdery,
porcelain-white
crescent,
reminiscent
of my mother's
sugar-coated
Christmas cookies,
hovers on
December's
dwindling day.

WINTER SAND

The moisture of this morning
burrows into my marrow.
A monotonous mist
rinses blacktop clean of snow.

The only memory
of our last storm,
the sander's dregs
at the side of the road.

Too dense to follow
the flow of water,
they lag behind,
cling to soles,
stow away
in the tread of a boot-heel,
in the cuff of my jeans,
in the crease of a paw.

MUD

It's moist, wet,
thick, and thirsty.
It smoothly, softly covers me.

It draws the poisons from within.
No one sees the me
beneath the crust
until it's hard and dry and thin,
until it turns to dust,
revealing silky, satin skin.

And it makes a mean pie
if you don't sling it.

ON THE LAST DAY OF THE FIRST MONTH

My dog and I,
we do not want
to leave the comfort
of the plaster and paint,
cinder and shingles of this place.

Scarved and gloved,
coated and leashed
we venture out.

The final wind of January
waits at the stoop
beneath the awning,
grabs my shoulders,
shakes his breath into my bones.

ALL I REALLY WANT

All I really want
is a little peace.

Not a piece of the rock
or a piece of the pie,
just a little peace of mind.

A place of peace
where noise is the rustle of leaves,
and a racket is the cracking
of acorns outside my window,

where I wake with sunlight,
dance naked with stars,
and only the deer and black bear
will witness.

A DIFFERENT VIEW

I live in this
hardscrabble town,
with its streets
of broken glass
and scents
of diesel fuel,

in a house
where the captain
of the Exxon Valdez
once slept,

where a bed
for the night
was worth thousands
when golfers came
to play the black.

Urbanites pluck
metropolitan roots
to escape to my soil,
soil suffocated
by insecticide
and cement.

My roots
seek comfort
farther north.

LEAVING LONG ISLAND

I'm just another someone on Secatogue,
Making my way through this hardscrabble haze.
I'm floating around in a Farmingdale fog,
Packing my things and counting the days.

Making my way through this hardscrabble haze,
I'm thinking of mountains, lakes, and trees,
Packing my things and counting the days,
Inhaling this sooty school bus breeze.

I'm thinking of mountains, lakes, and trees,
Dreaming of scents of pines and flowers,
Inhaling this sooty school bus breeze,
Filling up boxes and counting the hours.

Dreaming of scents of pines and flowers,
I'm floating around in a Farmingdale fog.
Filling up boxes and counting the hours,
I'm just another someone on Secatogue.

CLEANING DAY

This mad, sucking machine
is like some spoiled child
on a schoolyard swing,
incessantly nagging,
ordering,
Push! Push! Push!

And so I push,
maybe a bit too hard.
It unplugs itself from the wall.
It stalls, and I fall
headfirst into an army
of dusty-grey Easter bunnies,
high on Hoover fumes,
all egging me on
for the chase, and I race
into the plush, carpeted fields.

I've got a handle on it now,
and we plow,
headlong, headstrong,
through those energized bunnies
like some cotton pickers
pumped up on Duracells.

HANGING LAUNDRY

The lawn is damp
with dew,
and I am slippered,
in silence of dawn,
still in flannel and plaid.

My husband's Henley,
long outgrown,
envelops
my still-sleepy breast
in heather blue.

The grass,
her fingers the color
of hay and chlorophyll,
slides along soles
of drowsy feet,
seeps her way
through weaves of fiber,
searches for sun.

Finding skin,
she fondles each toe
with her wetness.

WITNESS

Two bodies cocooned
within cabin's timber tendrils.
Flames flutter and dance
upon the vastness of winter flesh,
mocking its whiteness.

Like the cold clenched fist
of an early April fern, I contract,
careful to conceal myself.
Fleece of English ivy,
my torso's coverlet.
My face half-hidden
by the brittle scaly fingers
of young white dormant oak
asleep in silence of solstice.

My breath reveals itself to glass.
They kiss, conspire to create
a mask of moisture
that blinds my eager passion.
Its skin now slick with sweat,
I dare not wipe away the fog
for windows often whisper
when they're touched.

YOU

You are the ecru sand
that slips through my fingers
on a warm summer day
at the beach.

In the cup of my hand
several grains of you linger,
only fragments of you
within reach.

You are the sultry salt air
that caresses my lips
on the bow of a boat
on the bay.

White whispers of you
tickle tongue's tip
while your spirit is
drifting away.

HUNGER

It begins
with a soft rumble.

I stir and sink
farther into
the comfort of down,
tighten the swollen,
fleshy sheaths
that shield my eyes
from light.

Angry now,
it howls
and grumbles,
startles me from sleep.

I spring straight up,
bolt from my bed
into the garden.

There I search
and find my sacrifice.
There I pluck
the perfect virgin peach.

EATING THE MANGO

First I poke
the oblong orb
to test the tenderness
within its satin skin.

Where ripeness
has devoured green
there is a vibrant blush,
a hint at what awaits beneath.

I pierce its armor sharply,
peel gently, reveal flesh
the color of September sunsets.

Teeth must take
the place of blade
to tear the thready meat
from bony pit.

I salivate.
I savor nectar tart,
yet sweet enough to satiate.

PEANUT BUTTER DREAMS

Oh how goes my heart aflutter
When I dream of peanut butter.
Upon arising, at daybreak,
I'll blend it with my breakfast shake.

I'll eat it morning, night, and noon
With finger, knife, or fork, or spoon.
Whether it be smooth or crunchy,
Perfect for my midday munchies.

Without a doubt the finest spread
On carrots, crackers, whole wheat bread.
Paired up with almost any jelly,
No finer comfort for my belly.

What better ending to my dream
Than peanut butter swirl ice cream?

BLUEBERRIES

A mere tickle
releases the grip
of the plumpest,
finest, ripest fruit.

Yet, a tug yields a crop
of hardened, reluctant,
too young marbles,
stony and sour.

Like the old spinster maid
who's never been touched
by the hand of a man,
a berry unpicked,
unchosen, turns grey.
It wrinkles and puckers,
loses appeal and fades away.

FIRE AND ICE

I am a cube of ice.
You, the soup
too hot to handle.
I cool you,
but the price –
I melt away.

I am the oxygen.
You, the
burning candle.
I feed you,
but the cost –
I am consumed.

GRANITE

Where rose thrives
beside stone
I bloom.

No room
for any human
save myself.

IN A DREAM

In a dream from a decade ago
he wears navy blue Big Yanks,
black boots, and a white v-neck shirt
with a pack of Pall Malls
rolled up in the sleeve
just above his bicep.

His hair is slicked back
with Brylcreem.
There's a cigarette
tucked behind his ear
and one in his mouth.

This night
I travel to a trailer park
in a small Kentucky town,
meet a man grown grey
as the smoke from his cigarettes,
grey as the screen
between him and my love.

With a rasping whisper,
a respirator reminds him
he is not alone.
Tubes thread into his nostrils,
cling to his arms, and he waits
for the comfortable stranger in white.

She checks vitals, doles out meds,
adjusts lifelines, with no more
than a mouthful of words
between them.

I remain here,
in a corner of his life,
a fly on the wall,
a woman he will never know.

MOTHER

In the hollow belly
of a dormant barbecue pit
there is a nest of feathers, twigs,
dried grass, and hay,
and three infant heartbeats–
until my husband pokes
at what he thinks is trash.

I intervene,
try to make it right,
return it to the way it was
before she left in search of food.
I leave walnuts, millet,
pumpkinseeds, and cashews
in a bowl on the porch,
my small apology.

She returns
to transplant her offspring.
Removes them, one by one,
by the scruffs of their necks,
takes them to a new home,
a home untouched by human hands,
returns them to the smell of earth.

I watch as she carries
the last one out,
pink and furless.
She stops to sniff,
fondles and kneads,
nuzzles and licks
her motionless baby.
He turns pale and cold.

THE SILENCE OF THE FLOWERS
(In memory of Bev Taylor)

She loved
the mountain laurel.
I think they loved her too.

It seems
they know
she is not here,

collectively deciding
not to bloom
as long
this year.

CONDOLENCE

If hearts
could bleed with pain
mine would
pour pools of sanguine rain.

I'd wallow in
your waves of weariness,
consumed by
oceans of your emptiness.

Swallowed by
your somber, sullen sea,
I'd drown in
tempered tides of empathy.

AFTERSHOCK
(For Evan Schwerner, NYPD, ESU Truck 4 and Bill Drewes, Jr., NYFD, Engine Co. 206)

Ground zero waits.
No hero in his mirror.
Just a soul in search of solace
from a senseless act of terror.
He showers, shaves, returns to what remains.

No time for tears or fear.
Anger pumps adrenaline,
good fuel for the fire
that he needs to fight the flames.
He showers, shaves, returns to what remains.

They've gone from search and rescue
to recover, desperate to discover
a gun, a badge, a body with a name.
He showers, shaves, returns to what remains.

Eyesight's blurred,
lungs are burned.
His leg is still infected,
but he doesn't feel the pain.
He showers, shaves, returns to what remains.

He's not feeling much these days,
digging through the smoldering haze.
No time to mourn a tarnished
silver skyline, scarred and stained.
He showers, shaves, returns to what remains.

STILL A BOY AT THIRTY-THREE

I call him cousin although he's not.
There is no blood between us here.
We built this bond, formed a clot
on common ground,
embracing the earth and the ether
that becomes us.

We saw through the bourbon haze
of smoky barrooms,
through the toughened skin
of our imposters.

I was too busy with myself to see,
through the sallow, grey shell,
this malignancy, this monster
that burrows into his tissue,
his blood, and his bones.
It drowns out his smiles,
his laughter. It buries a seed
within my cells.

The distance now measured
in miles and zones,
I'm panicked, anxious
to regain what we've lost.

I want to take him under my wing,
but feathers are not enough
to fend off his fate.

TOUGH AS TONY

You were the tough guy,
the macho member of the family
with your bleached-white
crew neck t-shirt with the rolled up sleeves
clinging to your brown Sicilian skin,
smoking those unfiltered cigarettes
and drinking Pop's homemade red.
His white was too much like moonshine,
you'd say, not enough texture and too much kick.

I watched chalky grey clouds of smoke
pour from your prominent nose
and always kept my distance.

I remember how cool that chain was,
dangling from your postman's pants,
and how cool you were
with your skin and your smoke
and your spirits, how tough you were.

I hated when you dunked me in the pool,
my pool, in my back yard
and kept my head under water
just long enough to be cool
without causing trouble.

I last saw you at your bedside,
your thick, jet-black hair
turned white, brittle, and sparse,
the lungs that fueled your mail routes
turned black with malignancy,
your once Sicilian skin turned sallow grey.

I wanted to tell you how much you meant to me
but could not break the silence
as I kissed your forehead,
said nothing as I left your house on 29th Street,
nothing as I lingered at your stoop.

I walked to Astoria Boulevard,
leaving behind my favorite uncle,
leaving behind my cool
and my last pack of Marlboros,
crumpled and broken.

THANKSGIVING, ROUTE 110 SOUTH

At the broken lines and blacktop
of Broad Hollow Road
a trio of crows gathers, reflecting light
like the satin skin of summer aubergine.
These carnivores, these cannibals,
they peck and claw
at chicken bones and biscuits,
scatter as traffic lights change
from red to green.
Feathered wings, burnt black in shade,
await the lull to carry their cargo
to the feast as we await the green.

Later we carnivores, we cannibals, we feast,
rip flesh from breast of turkey and goose,
shovel mounds of stuffing soaked in their blood
onto plates already too full,
drink Chablis and Chardonnay by the gallons.
As if not sated enough, we wait,
our wings clothed in cattle skin and fur,
for pastries and pies, cookies and cakes,
and we feast again.

There is an old woman,
her skin burnt brown by time.
She sits on a bench, at the curb
by the bus stop sign,
cloaked in her worn winter wool.
She nibbles and gnaws
at chicken bones and biscuits
where crows once gathered.

PROS AND CONS OF CHRISTMAS

Mistletoe and migraines
Starry lights and sleepless nights
Wrapping paper sprawled across the floor
Rapping neighbor's boom-box at my door

Red and silver Lionel caboose
Nestled underneath blue spruce
Tempting aromas of pfefferneuse
Aches and pains
And candy canes

Wassail, eggnog, hot holiday grog
The morning after mental fog
Spiral-cut pineapple honey-glazed hams
Department store lines and traffic jams

Searching the malls
For skateboards, board games
Searching my mind
For those reindeer names

Christmas Christians pack churches
To standing room only
And soup kitchens cater
To homeless and lonely

SHE LOVED ROSES
(In memory of my mother)

It shows in the shadows
of these walls,
in the nap
of the berber beneath me,
both similar shades
of her favorite hybrid.

The dresser and nightstand
of cherry mahogany
are outlined
in warm hues of her flower.

Even hydrangea heads
that gaze past the sill
of a northern window
display a tint
turned from lavender blue
to soft mauve
since she has gone.

Her image,
gowned in white,
framed in crystal,
cradles ivory blooms,
watches, watches me.

This day has come so soon,
too soon.
I stand at the mirror
in my pearls and purity.
Silver threads and promises
are all that hold me here.

LETTER TO MY FATHER

I sent you off to work that Monday morning,
assuring you everything would be all right.
You questioned the blueness of her lips,
the shadows on her skin,
and I sent you off to work.

I did not share my burden of bedpans,
the nights when bedside lanterns did not sleep,
my daily drives to Valhalla.

I sent you off to work that Monday morning.
I did not share the moment she muttered *mama*,
the moment my palm rested on the one small place
the malignancy had not yet discovered.
I did not share her final breath.

SILK SCARF

A black and white mosaic,
found wrinkled
and bunched up
at the back
of your cherry mahogany
dresser drawer.

It feels like you,
smells like you
and the 4711 cologne
Uncle Karl sent
from Schweinfurt
every Christmas.

Too delicate to be ironed,
it hangs in the bathroom
while I shower
so the steam
can kiss away the wrinkles
and make it young again.

If I wear this scarf
I will have to, one day,
wash it, wash away
your scent,
wash away
what's left of you.

MY MOTHER'S VASE

Crystal, clear upon my mantle
You carry, cradle, cuddle close.
At each side, a perfumed candle.
You hold the fragrance of a rose.

Towering over burning embers,
You bring a scent to things I remember.

IT'S JUST A BOX

A child's keepsake,
cardboard,
pale and frayed
at the corners.

Empty,
the gift it held
long outgrown.

This temporary trinket,
dented and discolored,
remains, reminding me of you.

Its emptiness intentional,
contents insignificant.

Like 1960's wall paper,
green and yellow
fade and blend
into themselves.
Lemon, lime,
olive, and buttercup
flowers, figures,
petals, and stems
sink into the bones of this box.

LOST REWARDS

I've lost so much
in these years that I've lived,
but my gains have multiplied.
Deposits made in a wisdom account,
my character is fortified.

I've lost so much
in these years that I've loved,
and my heart has paid the cost.
My spirit has earned the sweet rewards,
lessons of loves I have lost.

AFTER MIDNIGHT

My mouth
had never tasted this.
A sweet-as-sundae kiss,
so soft
my lips barely knew
they'd been touched.

I pray
my memory
will never fade enough
to fail this feeling.

A brush
of his breath
on my brow.
His velvet lips
against my face.

A kiss to caress;
a warm embrace.

A long enough pause
to excite
the surface of the skin,
to ignite
the incubation
of a stillborn sin.

REAL LOVE

No butterflies,
No goo-goo eyes.

No tongues that tie,
No need to lie.

No meals in bed
Since we were wed.

No need to touch
To know this much.

It's tried-and-true.
It's one from two.

A POEM FOR ROY

Ruby, rich, and radiant,
you are my
California cabernet.

Tart upon first taste,
you warm my flesh.
You flush my face.

You've grown mellow,
full, and smooth with age,
golden nectar of the sage.

With every sip
my lips are sated.
I am left inebriated.

MY HUSBAND

He knows
each fragile fear,

my many faces,
holds them dear.

He never
takes them out
in public places.

THESE ARE THE TIMES

Sometimes
I don't comb my hair.
I wear old clothes
and leave my face bare
just to see if he'll care.

Sometimes
I put on a pound
or two
just to see what he'll do.

Sometimes
I don't shower or shave,
for just a day,
just to see what he'll say.

Sometimes
I think,
no, I fear,
I just don't know
why he's here.

And
these are the times
he tells me
I'm beautiful.

THIS AUGUST NIGHT

Hazy, sallow, sunstruck clouds
do their dance of the veils
around an almost albino moon,
and I will dance for you,
barely in my summer sweat,
this steamy August night.

I will taste your salt.
It will satiate,
and what I cannot drink
will lick my skin
and keep me cool
this steamy August night.

Our flesh will skate and glide
on pulsing pools of passion.
Summer rapture
will ignite
the cool-fire
of this steamy August night.

A WEEKEND WITHOUT YOU

I will wake at dawn,
to Mozart and mantras.
No customary racket
of your bedside clock.

I will steep green tea leaves
with lotus blossom and bergamot.
No rush to brew Brazilian roast
in time for your rising.

I will soak in steamy scents
of lavender and sage.
No quick shower
in streams of lukewarm water.

I will sip champagne
from Hummingbird crystal.
No serenade of Budweiser belches
and pop top clicks.

I will dine
on sautéed shiitake mushrooms,
bok choy and brown rice.
My kitchen will not know
the smell of searing flesh.

I will burn incense
and sit cross-legged
on over-stuffed pillows,
with our dog at my side,
and see you in his eyes.

I will watch candle flames flicker
and wish them into kindling and cinders
and warm my solace by their fire.

I will read Sexton and Shakespeare
until their words sting my eyes
and seduce me into sleep.

I will climb the carpeted stairs
to the room with the queen-size bed,
and I will slip silently
into the empty space that is you.

Afterword

     Her work makes me remember what drew me to poetry in the first place – honest expression of intense emotion, encapsulated moments of shared human experience, careful personal reflections on the natural world, musical language. Reading her words has been a wonderful way to get to know her. It has been a pleasure to explore her inner landscapes. Many times I've found myself admiring her inventive perspectives and her delicate lyrical touch.

                      –Susan Astor, author of **Spider Lies**

About the Author

      In January 2000 Yolanda Coulaz signed up for a continuing education class entitled "You Can Write Poetry" offered by the Farmingdale Public Schools where she was named "Student of the Semester" for Spring 2002. Little did she know to what extent her instructor, Maxwell Corydon Wheat, Jr., would change her life. With his influence, guidance, and constant encouragement she has emerged as one of Long Island's most promising new poets.
      She is a member of the Performance Poets Association for which she has been a featured poet on many occasions. She is also a member of the Long Island Poetry Collective and the Live Poets Society. Her poetry has won awards from the Mid-Island YJCC, the Live Poets Society, the Lake Ronkonkoma Historical Society, and the Lathrop Senior Citizens Literary Society.
      Ms. Coulaz was named "Poet of the Month" in May 2002 at Partnersinverse.com where a collection of her nature photographs was featured along with a selection of her love poems.
      Spirits and Oxygen is her first book of poetry.